1 85103 048 4

First published 1988 by Editions Gallimard
First published 1989 in Great Britain by Moonlight Publishing Ltd,
131 Kensington Church Street, London W8
© 1988 Editions Gallimard
English text © Moonlight Publishing Ltd

Printed in Italy by La Editoriale Libraria

THE BOOK OF
DESERTS

DISCOVERERS

Written by Genevieve Dumaine
Illustrated by Sylvaine Perols

Translated by Penny Stanley-Baker

MOONLIGHT PUBLISHING

Contents

The magic of the desert	**8**
What is a desert?	**10**
Desert landscapes	**14**
The advancing desert	**16**
Wind and wilderness	**18**
Wind sculptures	**20**
A thirsty land	**22**
Hiding from the heat	**24**
Nomads	**26**
Settlers	**27**
Deserts of the world	**28-29**
Deserts of North America	**30**
Deserts of South America	**34**
Deserts of Central Asia	**38**
From Arabia to Sind	**44**
The sands of Arabia	**46**
The Sahara	**50**
When the Sahara was green	**56**
The Danakil Desert	**58**
The Namib	**60**
The Kalahari	**62**
The Australian deserts	**64**
The Antarctic	**68**
Reclaiming the desert	**70**
An A to Z of desert facts	**72**

The magic of the desert

A Pueblo Indian from New Mexico performing a rain dance.

The Hopi Indians of the Arizona desert use clay vessels in their religious ceremonies. The hole in the middle of this clay pot represents the hole in the earth out of which the Hopi first climbed from their underground world. The lines radiating from it are the souls of the unborn issuing from Mother Earth.

The word desert conjures up all sorts of different images. There is something magical and awe-inspiring about the sheer silence and desolation of a desert. It exposes man to the rigours of hunger and thirst. It tests his endurance and courage.

The Hebrews in the Bible spent many years wandering in the wilderness before they reached the Promised Land. So too, in the Muslim tradition,

> *Some wandered in the trackless desert and could not find their way to a city to live in. They were hungry and thirsty and had given up all hope.*
>
> Psalm 107, v.4

Jebel Ideid

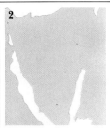

The Sinai Desert, which the Hebrews had to cross.

Jebel Musa and the monastery of St Catherine

the way to the sacred Watering Place lies across the desert.

No one is sure exactly which mountain in the Sinai Desert is Mount Sinai, where the Bible says God gave Moses the Ten Commandments. The most likely spot is Jebel Musa, where the monastery of Catherine now stands, but recently traces of the Hebrews' wanderings have been found in Jebel Ideid, much further north.

At dawn, the witch-doctor interprets the prints left by the 'pale fox', a jackal, in the magic square of sand.

> *They did not care about me, even though I rescued them from Egypt and led them through the wilderness: a land of deserts and sand-dunes, a dry and dangerous land, where no one lives and no one will even travel.*
>
> Jeremiah 2, v.6

9

What is a desert?

Some deserts, like the Arizona desert in the USA, are covered by a thin coat of snow in winter.

The word 'desert' comes from the Latin, meaning deserted or abandoned – a place hostile to all form of life.

Deserts form wherever rain-bearing clouds encounter some sort of obstacle that prevents them from shedding their water. These obstacles produce four main types of desert.

Tropical deserts are caused by belts of high pressure over the tropics. These form a cushion of hot, dry air which the rain-bearing clouds cannot penetrate. As a result, at the same latitude on every continent there is a desert belt.

Coastal deserts are due to cold ocean currents along western coasts. These lower the temperature of the winds blowing in off the sea, which then hold far less moisture. Sometimes mist is

blown in but it seldom condenses to give rain.

Inland deserts, such as the Gobi in Mongolia or the Gibson in Australia, are so far from the coast that sea-winds have to travel vast distances to reach them, and in the process lose all their moisture. The heart of major continents, such as Asia and Australia, is often arid.

Rain-shadow deserts, such as the Takla Makan in China, form when mountain ranges lie in the path of moist winds blowing in off the sea. As the air rises over the high ground, it expands and cools, and the moisture it carries condenses, to fall as rain or snow. The side of the mountain range nearest to the coast receives all the rain; the other side gets none.

The desert floor is often cracked and flawed. There is no moisture to bind the soil together.

Many of the most typical features of a desert can be seen in this Saharan scene: sand-dunes, many-coloured rocks, loose boulders and, in the distance, an oasis.

High up, the air is thin, cold and dry. The Himalayan plains are cold deserts.

In the Sahara, the nights are cold, with even an occasional touch of frost. The air is so clear that the moonlight is dazzling.

In temperate zones, clouds affect the temperature. During the day they stop the full heat of the sun getting through. At night they prevent the accumulated heat of the earth escaping (**1**). In the desert, though, the scorching air cools very fast at night because there are no clouds to stop the hot air rising (**2**).

Deserts can be cold as well as hot.

The climate of a desert is determined by two factors: its height in relation to sea-level (altitude), and its distance from the Equator (latitude). The Sahara in North Africa and the Atacama in Chile are both extremely hot; they are low-lying and close to the Equator. By contrast, winters in the Gobi Desert in Mongolia, which is further north and at a higher altitude (1,200 m), are very severe, with temperatures reaching -50°C!

Scorching days, freezing nights

In desert regions, the dry air gives no protection against the sun's rays, and during the day the temperature can rise rapidly to 70°C (54°C in the shade).

However, when the sun goes down the earth soon loses its heat, and the

temperature falls again rapidly, sometimes to below zero. Without the welcome coolness of the night, few plants or animals would survive.

On a bright, cold, eerie moonlit
night in the Sahara, the sand
looks as white as snow.

Desert landscapes

Great plateaux of bare rock are a common desert feature: black basalt in Syria, limestone in the Hadhramaut, sandstone in the Tassili (on the fringes of the Sahara).

The reg is made up of a mixture of tiny stones, formed when the bedrock cracked (1) or exploded (2). Some are stained dark by metallic salts, others have been polished to a deep sheen by the wind-blown sand (3).

Deserts are not always sandy. Wind, frost and extreme temperatures erode and sculpt the landscape into spectacular shapes: steep cliffs, great mounds of boulders, craggy mountains, bare rock of startling colours.

The nature of the landscape is determined by the geological

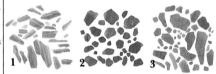

1   2   3

composition of the bedrock, or of the soil. High, arid plateaux strewn with rocks and boulders (*hamadas*), gravelly plains (*regs*) or volcanic mountain ranges are in fact more common than the rolling sand-dunes we usually associate with deserts.

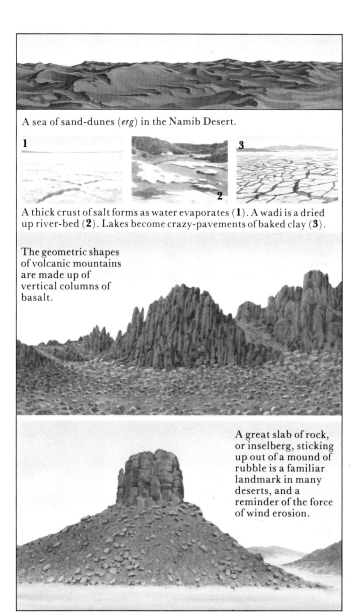

A sea of sand-dunes (*erg*) in the Namib Desert.

A thick crust of salt forms as water evaporates (**1**). A wadi is a dried up river-bed (**2**). Lakes become crazy-pavements of baked clay (**3**).

The geometric shapes of volcanic mountains are made up of vertical columns of basalt.

A great slab of rock, or inselberg, sticking up out of a mound of rubble is a familiar landmark in many deserts, and a reminder of the force of wind erosion.

15

The advancing desert

The people of the Sahel are forced to dig ever deeper in search of water.

Cattle need 30 litres of water a day. As the drought spreads, the pools and wells run dry, and their bones litter the landscape.

The great deserts of the world have existed since prehistoric times. Then, as now, they were constantly shifting in response to changes in the climate.

The Sahel, the southern fringe of the Sahara, was first settled in neolithic times. As the desert advanced or retreated over time the people who made a scant living in these border lands moved too. But now the desert is expanding so fast that many people have to flee in order to survive.

Desertification, or desert advance, is due both to man's intervention and to natural causes. The climatic changes are gradual, occurring in cycles of 10 to 1000 years. Minute variations in the Earth's orbit affect the temperature of the Earth's atmosphere, which in turn determines wind and rainfall. Rainfall varies more quickly, perhaps within 10 years. It is linked to a recurring warm ocean current in the Pacific, 'el Niño', which influences the monsoons and trade winds.

Twenty thousand years ago the Sahel was part of a huge desert which extended 400 km further south. What we see happening now is the desert reverting to its former boundaries.

In drought-prone areas men have made matters worse. By raising crops

and livestock they disturb the natural vegetation. By felling large numbers of trees they remove a major source of humidity from the atmosphere. In certain areas overgrazing destroys pasture land, and lowers the level of the water table. In no time at all the desert moves in.

The felling of trees lets the desert in.

Driven by the wind, the sand-dunes advance relentlessly to engulf both fields and crops.

In the Nordest Desert in Brazil, the soil has dried to a hard, baked crust where once the forest stood.

17

Wind and wilderness

The alluvial deposits on dried-up river-beds are gradually sifted by the wind, which blows away the finest particles (1) until only the larger stones remain (2) as a bed of gravel (3). The regs (4) or gravelly plains, are a result of this gradual sifting process.

The wind blows away the finer particles in great clouds of sand and dust.

In desert regions there are few trees or plants to check the wind in its course. Nor is there any moisture to bind the different elements of the soil together. The finest and lightest of these are blown away by the constant and often violent winds which rake the earth. This sifting process is known as wind erosion. The wind teases grains of sand and small stones out from

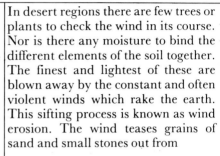

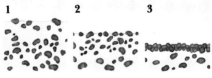

amongst larger ones, rolling or bouncing them along before it. In its wake, it leaves a bed of gravel (a *reg*), or an expanse of bare rock (a *hamada*).

Winds carry.
Strong winds sometimes raise huge clouds of suffocating dust and sand, which can blot out the sun altogether. Desert sandstorms can be fatal to both

man and beast. The dust and sand swept up in the strong wind are often carried thousands of miles over sea or land before falling to earth once more.

A sandstorm brewing in the Arizona Desert sends these Navajo children running to safety.

Winds erode.
Wind-blown sand constantly eats away at the desert rock. It rounds and shines pebbles, etches lines in the rock-face, sculpts boulders, and

In a storm, the camel closes its nostrils to keep out the whirling sand.

carves out caves in narrow rocky gorges. The combined forces of wind and sand are like a giant sanding-machine, continuously modelling the landscape.

A succession of dunes is known as the *erg*. All sand-dunes are asymmetric; the side facing the wind is a gentle slope, the sheltered side is steep.

Winds deposit.
When the wind slackens in pace or comes up against an obstacle, it deposits its load of sand. Wherever there is any vegetation, the sand is distributed evenly over a wide area, forming a sandy plain or *goze* – the Iranian word. More often than not, the sand accumulates in dunes. These may either be odd, isolated dunes, or a succession of undulating dunes.

19

Wind sculptures

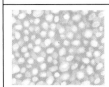

Grains of sand are tiny pieces of solid quartz, which become rounded and polished as the wind rubs them together.

The desert wind carves out the landscape.

The contours of the desert are shaped by the wind, as it eats away at the layers of soft rock, or deposits its load of sand on the dunes. The outlines are determined by the strength, direction and constancy of the wind. The names may vary from one country to the next, but the outlines are the same.

Barchan

In areas where sand is scarce, the wind blows it into individual, crescent-shaped dunes, called *barchans*. These shift constantly as the wind direction changes.

Mushroom rock

Because the wind seldom lifts the sand more than one or two metres above the ground, rocks are worn away at the base only. They develop curious mushroom shapes, with rounded tops balanced on narrow stems.

Yardang

In chalk or clay country, where the soil is soft, the wind often carves out little crested humps. These *yardangs* are typical of the deserts of Turkestan and Iran. They all face the same way, into the prevailing wind.

Seif

Seifs, or 'S'-shaped dunes, are formed when the wind blows from opposite directions, turning a line of barchans inside out. *Seif* is the Arabic word for a curved sword.

Star-shaped dune

Star-shaped dunes like these are a sign of changeable winds. This type of dune may be 300 m high, and does not shift when the wind changes. In the wind, sand rises from the crest of the dune like a plume of smoke.

Parallel dunes

Strong, constant winds form long, parallel dunes, which sometimes extend over 200 km. The straight corridors between the dunes are clear of sand, and make natural roads for caravans or trucks.

A thirsty land

The sand-grouse soaks its feathers so that its chicks can suck the water from them.

On foggy nights, the darkling beetle of the Namib Desert leans forward so that the drops of water forming on its back trickle down into its mouth.

This desert-vine, which grows in the

Namib, and the colocynth, or bitter-apple, of the Sahara are both precious sources of water.

Water may be scarce, but it is present in different forms in the desert. There are the occasional rains, the moisture in the night air, and the underground

Tap-roots Bulbs   Shallow roots   Cactus

sheets of stagnant water. It is enough to enable some types of animal and plant life to subsist. But for survival, every droplet of water must be pain-stakingly saved and put to good use.

Finding water

Some plants send down tap-roots as deep as 40 m, in search of water. Others have widespread, shallow roots, which trap rain and dew near the sur-face, and also secrete toxins to kill off seedlings nearby which try to take root.

At night, sea fog rolls in over the Atacama Desert in Chile, and the Namib on the West African coast.

Carnivores, such as scorpions, reptiles and foxes, get all the water they need from their prey. Herbivores, like the addax and the gerbil, survive on the moisture in seeds, juicy plants or dew-soaked leaves.

Storing water

Camels can drink up to 100 litres of water at a time, which they then store in the fatty tissue of their hump. They can go a full month without drinking.

Certain plants store enough water in their root-systems, or in their stems or trunks (the cactus-stem is a sort of sponge), to last several years.

Saving water

Many desert plants are small, hard and compact, with thick waterproof coatings which prevent water escaping and evaporating in the heat. Their prickly leaves protect them against predators. Animals slow down their metabolic rate in the heat, and their droppings are hard and dry, because the moisture in their food is all absorbed.Animals sheltering in burrows stop up the entrances, so that any moisture they breathe out can be trapped and re-used.

It is not the earth, but the water which brings forth the fruit.

Turkmen proverb

Torrential rain revives plants and animals alike.

The addax, or desert antelope, can survive for long spells without drinking. Plants provide it with moisture.

An irrigation well in the Sahara.

23

Hiding from the heat

This African squirrel is using its tail as a sunshade.

The huge ears of the fennec, or desert fox, help it to keep cool.

Most insects spend the day in burrows underground.

The skink, a tiny lizard, can burrow down out of sight in a second.

All living creatures need to maintain a constant body-temperature. Getting too hot or too cold can be fatal. In the desert, both people and animals have to lead a largely nocturnal existence, seeking shade during the long hot hours of the day.

Some animals shelter in underground burrows. Others are protected by a hard shell, a scaly skin or a good thick coat.

Many mammals, more vulnerable than insects or reptiles, have large ears which catch any cooling breezes. They also increase the surface area of their bodies so that they can lose heat more rapidly.

Lizards and tortoises survive temperatures of up to 50°C by sheltering under a bush (1). Insects and small mammals dig burrows for themselves; one metre below ground, the temperature drops to 30°C (2). Gliding birds, like the vulture, escape the heat by flying high above the land. At 300m, the temperature is only 27°C (3).

Ostriches and camels are both tall and have long, thin necks; their heads are well above the ground, where the temperature is some 10°C cooler (4).

Desert-dwelling people shelter from the heat of the day under cover in their camps, and wear loose, flowing garments to keep cool.

A pair of beady eyes protrude above the sand – the horned viper lying in wait.

Nomads

The people of the desert have had to adapt their way of life to the arid land. Many desert-dwellers are nomads, travelling people who move on from place to place in search of new supplies of water and salt, and fresh grazing for their animals. Their dwellings are very light so that they are easy to take down and move. Despite the encroachment of modern civilisation many tribes still keep to their ancient way of life.

Hunters and gatherers

The Australian Aborigines and the South African Bushmen are nomadic peoples who have adapted totally to their desert environment. They do not try to raise animals or cultivate the arid land. Instead, they hunt wild animals and search out plants and roots. They live in makeshift shelters made of twigs and greenery.

The Tuareg live in the middle of the Sahara Desert. Their tents are made from the hides and skins of the camels, goats, sheep and cows they raise.

The inhabitants of the cold deserts of Central Asia live in round tents made of felt, called yurts, which can be dismantled rapidly.

The Australian Aborigines used to move around in small family groups from one waterhole to the next.

Settlers

In Morocco, many of the oasis-towns which flank the valleys of the Northern Sahara are built of dried earth, and are fortified to withstand attack.

The towns of the Yemen are built of stone and earth. The tall, white-washed houses cluster together on rocky hilltops.

In the Arizona Desert, the Navajo Indians used to pass the winter in solidly constructed mud-dwellings called hougans.

Not all desert people are nomads. Some settled where there is a permanent supply of water. The architecture of their towns and villages is often spectacular. In many places modern methods of irrigation have made it possible for gardens and crops to flourish in the middle of the desert.

The Indians of the American deserts have to contend with blistering heat during the summer months, and bitterly cold, snowy winters. Both the Hopi and the Navajo Indians live in settlements. Some have houses built of stone, while others live in shacks. The Pueblo Indians have carved whole fortress-towns for themselves out of the solid rock.

Deserts of the world

1. Great Basin
2. Death Valley
3. Mojave

9. Sahara

10. Nubian

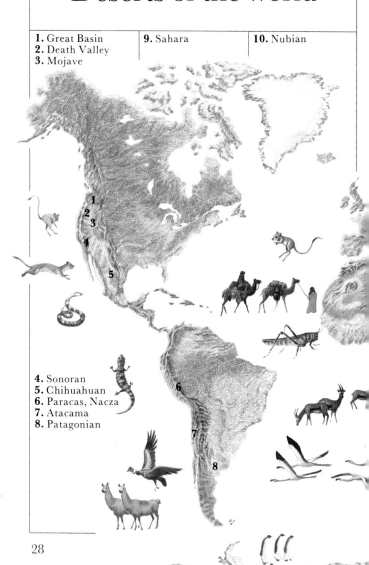

4. Sonoran
5. Chihuahuan
6. Paracas, Nacza
7. Atacama
8. Patagonian

11. Danakil
12. Namib
13. Kalahari
14. Great Nafud
15. Nedjed
16. Rub 'al Khali
17. Hadhramaut
18. Hejaz
19. Negev

20. Dasht-e Kavir
21. Dasht-e Lut
22. Kara Kum
23. Thar
24. Kyzyl Kum
25. Takla Makan
26. Gobi

27. Great Sandy Desert
28. Gibson
29. Nullarbor
30. Simpson
31. Great Victoria
32. Sturt
33. Antarctic

Deserts of North America

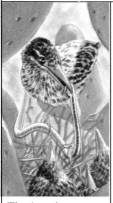

The American roadrunner seldom takes to the air. This member of the cuckoo family hunts lizards and snakes, which it stabs with its beak.

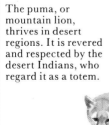

The puma, or mountain lion, thrives in desert regions. It is revered and respected by the desert Indians, who regard it as a totem.

Between the Rockies and the mountain ranges, or sierras, along the Pacific Coast, a succession of deserts stretches right down to Mexico. In this region, rainfall is scarce. Mountain peaks rise abruptly from rocky plains, ravines and deep canyons cut deep into the high plateaux. Here and there, white dunes of powdery chalk, salt lakes and extinct volcanoes stand out against the rugged background.

The Great Salt Lake of Utah is all that remains of a huge lake which once covered the entire Great Basin Desert. On this desolate plateau the greyish-green sagebrush, a mountain shrub, grows alongside the desert cactus.

Death Valley lies some 80 m below sea-level, a narrow corridor strewn with rocky debris and constantly shifting sand-dunes. Temperatures of 57°C in the shade have been recorded there.

Pungent creosote bushes grow in scattered clumps all over the Mojave Desert. The roots of this bush secrete a toxin into the soil, discouraging other plants from growing alongside.

The Sonoran Desert on the Gulf of California is noted for its many different types of cactus, including the giant barrel and saguaro. These provide shelter and food for a great variety of wildlife, including the strange coati, a member of the raccoon family.

The Chihuahuan Desert lies between the two Sierra Madre ranges.

These fairy-tale towers carved out by the wind stand in the Painted Desert, which owes its name to the extraordinary colours of its rocks.

After a shower of rain, the Californian desert bursts into bloom.

The seeds of these ephemeral (short-lived) plants lie dormant in the soil throughout the longest drought. Their tough outer skins only open when there is enough rain to ensure completion of their life-cycle. Some plants germinate and flower in the space of a single day.

Plants growing on the floor of the canyon, where there is more moisture, often survive for several months at a stretch.

Some Navajo women still hunt on horseback in traditional costume.

Pueblo Indians used to calculate the time of year from the midday sun. The sun's rays, passing through a series of narrow cracks in blocks of stone, fell upon a spiral engraved on the rock below. By observing the position of the rays on the spiral, the people knew when it was time to sow or harvest their crops.

Cactus country

Many North American deserts are studded with cactus plants. There are no less than 140 different species of cacti, from the tiny 5 cm nipple cactus, to the towering saguaro which grows 15 m high and can live up to 200 years. Desert creatures feast on the juicy, sugary fruit, and then obligingly disperse the seed far and wide in their droppings, so that there are always plenty of new cactus plants.

Desert flowers are brightly coloured and strongly scented, to attract the animals which pollinate them.

1. Spring equinox
2. Summer solstice
3. Autumn equinox
4. Winter solstice

1   2   3   4

The living desert

A surprising number of animals manage to survive in the desert. Most are nocturnal in habit. The kangaroo-rat is particularly well adapted to its hostile environment, and has even made its home in Death Valley. It never has a drink; it gets the moisture it needs from eating seeds which it stores underground in its burrow until they have soaked up the moisture from the soil. In the intense heat of summer, the Mojave squirrel retreats to the cool of its burrow, lowering its metabolic rate to conserve energy.

Some Indians, such as the Hopis and the Navajos, still live on reserves in the North American deserts. The Pueblo Indians live in remote and inaccessible villages hollowed out of the cliff-face.

The water in this pool in Death Valley evaporated long ago..

The elf-owl makes its nest in the huge saguaro cactus.

The fleshy prickly-pear cactus is a source of precious food and water for the antelope squirrel.

The deserts of South America

A wide belt of desert stretches right across South America, from the coasts of Peru and Chile in the north, down to the Atlantic shores of the south.

Coastal deserts

The icy Humboldt Current flows northwards along the west coast of South America for some 3,000 km, giving rise to cold, dry onshore winds. These collect moisture over the warmer coastal plains, then rise over the Andes. The moisture condenses, shrouding the coastal region for most of the

Lamas provide wool, meat and a means of transport. Like their relation the camel they are well adapted to both drought and extreme cold.

The Paracas Desert

year in dense mist. Nevertheless, high evaporation keeps the soil very dry.

The Paracas Desert, near Lima, is famous for its tall, pastel-coloured dunes, in differing shades of white, pink and green.

The Atacama Desert in Chile is the driest of all the world's deserts. Some parts have never seen rain. However, in the last hundred years the high plains have become a valuable source of gold, silver, iodine and copper.

Pelicans gather on the desert shores to fish.

Candelabra cacti grow on the wetter slopes.

The Atacama Desert

Much of the copper is taken from open-cast mines.

Mysterious mummies guard the fringes of the Paracas Desert.

The mummies are draped in a magnificent funeral cloth, or *fardo*. It consists of several pieces of cloth woven in continuous strips, 28 m long and 4 m wide. The weaving of each one required two single strands of thread, 160 km in length!

In pre-Columbian times, there were no wheels or spools on which to wind the thread. Instead it was laid out flat, full-length, on the vast open stretches of the Nazca Desert.

Signs and symbols in the desert of Nazca

Near the towns of Paracas and Nazca in Peru, not far from the Pacific coast, a series of long, absolutely straight lines appears to have been cut into the high stony plain. Here and there, on the slopes of neighbouring hills, huge stylised drawings of birds and beasts have been etched in the rock. In the sandier stretches of the desert, as the wind shifts, it may uncover ancient mummies swathed in funeral garments and surrounded by clay utensils. There has been no rain to wash away these traces of a civilization which probably goes back to 500 or even 800 BC. Archaeologists suggest that this ancient unknown race of people used the long straight grooves in the desert to lay out and stretch the kilometres of unbroken thread from which their ceremonial funeral robes were made.

Pelican, 105 m

36

Condor, 135 m   Spider, 46 m

The port of Ushuaia, on Tierra del Fuego, is the southernmost town in the world.

These line-drawings, which also feature on funeral vases, must have held some magic significance.

The Patagonian Desert

This desert stretches from South Argentina to Tierra del Fuego. It lies in the lee of the Andes, which absorb any rain coming from the west. Dry, grassy steppelands give way to vast flat stretches of bare pampas, swept by an icy wind known as the *pampero*. Here and there, a thorn-bush or tuft of grass breaks the monotony of black earth, sand and scree. The further south, the colder the desert becomes, and the sparser the vegetation. Only lichen and thistles survive in the bitter cold. Long trailing clouds move across the vast expanse of deep blue sky, but they seldom bring rain.

Glaciers form high above the snow-line in the mountains, when the layers of snow are gradually compressed into these rivers of ice which creep slowly downhill. The southern tip of the Patagonian Desert is a mass of glaciers.

37

The deserts of Central Asia

Cobra poised to strike

The white saxaul trees lose their leaves in the heat of summer.

Central Asia extends all the way from the Caspian Sea to Mongolia. This vast area, far removed from any ocean, and hemmed in by the high Himalayan Mountains, comprises a string of deserts where conditions are particularly harsh. In the torrid heat of summer the air is heavy with dust, whereas in winter icy winds blowing in from the Arctic bring flurries of snow. Plants and animals have had to adapt to these extreme conditions. Animals spend much of the year under cover keeping to a state of semi-hibernation, emerging in the spring.

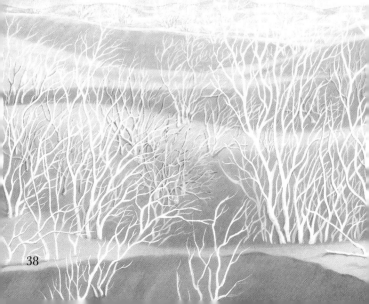

Bactrian, or two-humped, camels originate from these parts.

The Turkestan Desert is the fourth largest in the world, one-fifth as big as the Sahara. Two rivers cross this vast area, splitting it into a series of deserts. The Kara Kum (meaning 'black sands'), between the Aral Sea and the Amu Darya River, is a succession of sandy hills sprinkled with saxaul trees, and treacherous, shifting *barchan* dunes. The Kyzyl Kum ('red sands') is a much smaller desert, wedged between the Amu and Syr Darya Rivers. It is a patchwork of red sandy plains, rocky mountains, and plateaux of sand and shale.

Clumps of giant fennel provide shelter for birds.

Whenever rain falls, mushrooms spring up overnight.

The wild donkey, or *Kulan*, is now a protected species and increasing in number in Russian Turkestan.

Chinese Turkestan

The Tarim Basin in China contains a vast area of sand almost twice the size of the United Kingdom: the Takla Makan Desert. The name means 'place of no return'. The mountainous areas bordering the desert were once dotted with oases, which were staging-posts for caravans travelling the Silk Road. Many of these have since vanished beneath the shifting sands. The Takla Makan is a mixture of undulating dunes and deep basins of dried-up clay, known as *bayirs*. The water in the few remaining pools is salty. Entire caravans have disappeared without trace in the devastating storms that sweep this desert. Now and then a heap of dry bones is uncovered – a reminder of the toll the desert takes on human life. The heart of the Takla Makan has only recently become accessible by helicopter.

The ruined city of Lou-Lan, on Lake Lop Nor, was once a staging-post.

The desert hedgehog lives on a diet of insects.

The ruins of ancient fortresses are gradually eroded by wind and sand as the desert sweeps in.

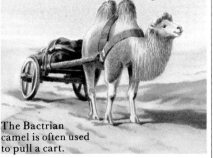

The Bactrian camel is often used to pull a cart.

Nomads ignore the frontier in the icy wastes between Pakistan and China.

Shepherds on both sides of the border dress warmly against the cold.

Further east, the deserts become increasingly cold. The Gobi Desert in Mongolia is a huge area of arid steppe, blasted by freezing wind. There are no rivers, streams or lakes, only a few pools of stagnant water left by the infrequent rains. The ground is often stony, with here and there a few clumps of coarse grass. The nomads of these plains live in yurts, the round tents made of felt pictured on page 26.

The Himalayan plateaux to the north of India are high-altitude deserts. High up, the air becomes thinner and the temperature falls, thereby causing a dramatic drop in the level of humidity. There is practically

About 2,000 years ago, this weather-beaten mass of stone was a watch-tower.

Camel caravans still travel the ancient Silk Road.

In the Gobi Desert, there are only a few sparse tufts for the horses to graze.

no precipitation in these lands on the roof of the world. The salt in any remaining water is concentrated by evaporation. Strong winds strip the rock bare, making it impossible for plants to take root.

The inhabitants of these areas live largely in the valleys, which are often irrigated. They keep yaks, small ponies and sheep, all of which are well adapted to the inhospitable climate.

Buddhist temples and shrines look out from the bleak hill-tops.

From Arabia to Sind

Qanats are man-made underground canals. The water which collects in them is brought to the surface through

well-shafts. Invented by the Persians 3,000 years ago, qanats are still in use in Pakistan and North Africa.

The Sahara extends beyond the Red Sea into Asia, reaching east along the Tropic of Cancer. This stretch of hot desert runs from Arabia all the way to the Sind, in India, with very little variation in climate, vegetation or wildlife.

Persian merchants, setting forth on their travels, have to cross vast expanses of desert, barren sandy wastes where there is neither grass, nor any form of vegetation for their horses to feed on …
Marco Polo

Baluchi nomads pitch their tents in the foothills, where there is grazing for their flocks.

In the Thar Desert, people still come from far and wide to attend the traditional camel-market.

In villages like this one in the Iranian Desert, the mud houses are built close together. Their thick walls keep out the heat.

The great Iranian Desert extends into Afghanistan and Pakistan. It consists of the Dasht-e Kavir, a vast salt desert, and the Dasht-e Lut, with its towering sand dunes over 300 m high. A fierce wind blows the sand into great furrows called *kaluts*, 20 to 30 m wide. The high mountains surrounding this area bring about some humidity.

The hottest and most arid of the eastern deserts is the *Thar*, in north-west India. Caravans bearing salt, wool and skins do not even attempt to cross it in the heat of the day.

Oil gushes from the ground in the Zagros Mountains of Khuzestan, in Iran. It is exported all over the world.

The sands of Arabia

One-third of the entire Arabian peninsula is covered by sand-dunes.

A modern motorway system linking the major Saudi cities patterns the desert sands.

To the north lies the Great Nafud, where the *simoom*, a hot, gusty wind, raises great clouds of fine yellow dust. Further south is the Nedjed, a sun-baked rocky plateau of lava and granite. East of the Nedjed stretches the Rub 'al Khali, or 'empty quarter', a barren sandy waste, parts of which are still unexplored. The Hadhramaut is a limestone plateau scored with deep canyons; its name means 'all vegetation is dead'. Only the valleys of the Hadhramaut are inhabited.

The discovery of oil has brought modern technology to the Hejaz, revolutionising the life-style of its inhabitants. Also in this desert lie the sacred cities of Islam. At its heart is Mecca, birthplace of Muhammad.

The sacred shrine, or Kaaba, is a cube-shaped building draped in an enormous black cloth embroidered in gold. Inside it is the Black Stone, which, according to legend, was given to Adam on banishment from Eden. Once white, it has been blackened by the sins of the pilgrims who kiss and touch it, before walking seven times round the Kaaba to obtain forgiveness.

Each year almost 3 million Muslims go on pilgrimage to the sacred shrine at Mecca.

This telephone standing in the middle of the desert is powered by solar energy.

Riyadh, capital of Saudi Arabia

There is so much salt in the Dead Sea that it crystallises and floats to the surface.

These pyramids at Merowe, in the Nubian Desert, are remnants of the ancient kingdom of Kush, which disappeared in the fourth century BC.

The Arabian Desert reaches north into Syria and encompasses Palestine and India. The landscape is a mixture of sandy dunes, rocky plateaux and craggy peaks; the colours are russet reds and ochres.

The **Negev Desert**, a vast triangle extending south to the Dead Sea, was once a green and fertile land. Over two thousand years ago the Nabataeans succeeded in irrigating it by using a complex network of underground drains and canals. The capital Petra was extremely prosperous. But the people were conquered by the Romans, and Muslim nomads subsequently moved in with their flocks; the area then reverted to desert. At present the Israelis are attempting to restore the ancient water-cisterns, wells and canals, in order to establish plantations of young trees.

The rose of Jericho is a typical example of the plants that grow in the deserts of Arabia, Syria and Palestine. It grows into a small bush with short, velvety branches. Once the berries ripen, the plant rolls up into a tight round ball. The wind sends it scuttling to and fro across the sand, until it finally comes to rest in a damp spot where it can once more put down roots.

The water in the Dead Sea contains sulphur; it is bitter and toxic.

In the lonely wastes of the deserts, the domed roof of a mosque calls passing nomads to prayer.

The ancient city of Petra (the name means 'stone') was hewn out of solid rock at the foot of a deep gorge in Jordan.

49

The Sahara

The Arabic word *sahra* means 'wilderness'. It is the name given to the vast area of desert extending from the Atlantic in the west to the Red Sea in the east, from the Mediterranean in the north right down into Africa.

The Sahara is roughly the size of the USA and encompasses ten different countries. It is the only tropical desert to extend as far as the Tropic of Cancer. Rain falls infrequently but heavily on the northern fringes in

A pinnacle of phonolite lava in the Ahaggar Mountains.

The fennec, or desert fox

The making of three cups of tea is a ritual gesture of hospitality amongst nomadic tribes.

winter, and in the south in summer. What moisture there is rapidly evaporates in the heat; ground temperature can rise above 70°C (55° in the shade). But the nights are cold, and winter frosts are common.

The winds in the Sahara tend to be strong and unpredictable. They blow up suddenly into sandstorms, leaving a trail of destruction in their wake. Most well-known are the *khamsin*, the *guebli* and the *harmattan*.

The Sahara is a mixture of different land formations, caused by geological movement breaking up and reshaping the original crystalline substratum, with its covering of lime and sandstone. Volcanic activity and erosion have also varied the contours of the landscape. The **mountains** may be a solitary peak or a whole region of mountains (Ahaggar, Iforas, Aïr, Tibesti). Of all the Saharan land-forms, the **reg** is the most common. Vegetation and wildlife are scarce and nomads seldom set foot there. The **erg**, undulating, shifting sand-dunes, is the landscape often associated with the Sahara. In fact, only one-fifth of it is erg.

The Sahara can be divided geographically into separate sections.

The **Northern Sahara** is an area of oases; palm-trees grow along former river-beds. The architecture is austere and quite distinctive. The nomads here are of Arab extraction.

The River Niger flows out to sea through the desert between Timbuktu and Gao.

Fossilized tree-trunks over 200 million years old are uncovered by the wind.

The dunes are spectacular, but not the most typical landscape of the Sahara.

In the **Central Sahara** lie the **Ahaggar Mountains** (Hoggar, in Arabic), which rise from a succession of plateaux, the **Tassili**.

The Ahaggar massif is a mixture of high mountains, with the occasional jagged peak of volcanic lava soaring above the rest (Atakor, 3,500 m), and steep-sided valleys where enough water collects for some wildlife to survive. There are no palm-trees, but acacias and cypresses grow in these valleys which are home to the Tuareg, a proud feudal people of Berber origin, renowned for their customs and traditions.

Flocks of ostriches were once common in the Sahara, but nowadays only a few solitary birds live around Aïr.

Gerbils do not drink. They obtain all the moisture they need from the seeds they eat.

Desert sand is very fertile. A little water will germinate the seeds lying dormant in the sand.

The most typical desert scenery is a mixture of sand and stones.

The **Tassili** are high plateaux intersected by steep-sided ravines several hundred metres deep. The relentless process of erosion has gradually whittled away the rock, leaving ridges of needle-sharp peaks.

The **Southern Sahara** is an area of vast regs and isolated high massifs (**Aïr, Tibesti** and **Ennedi**). The highest peak in the Sahara is Emi Koussi (3,415 m), an outcrop of volcanic rock in the Tibesti.

The nomadic Berber tribes, the Tuareg, the Tebu and the Moors, travel with their camels as far south as the Sahel, in search of the precious camel-grass which only grows where there is rain.

The **Atlantic Sahara** is less arid because a cold sea-current flows up the coast from the Canary Islands, bringing both fog and dew. Nomadic tribes of Moors constantly cross this region on their way between Morocco and Senegal. The coast is peopled with tribes of fishermen.

The Sahara is a crossroads, where people of different races and religions come together. The people of the oases, such as the Haratin, are of Negro descent. In the north, both nomads and settlers are of Arab origin, whereas the mountains are home to the Berber tribes.

Oases, fringed with date-bearing palm-trees, are paradises of greenery in the desert wastes.

The cheetah's spots are perfect camouflage against a background of sand and stone. This animal has become increasingly rare.

Migratory locusts descend in clouds, devouring everything in sight.

Salt is a vital commodity in the desert for both man and beast. Once a year, the nomads take their herds to the brine-pits to lick the salt.

Once the Sahara was green.

The Ténéré, a plateau north of the Tibesti Mountains, is now completely deserted. However, traces of ancient villages have been found there, together with a number of stone tools, bone harpoons, arrowheads, and weights for fishing-nets.

In prehistoric times, some 6,000 years ago, the Sahara was far greener and wetter than now. Archaeologists and geologists have been able to piece together a picture of life in those days. The bones of crocodiles and hippopotami have been found in the beds of dried-up lakes, together with the remains of fish and molluscs. Traces of pollen from lime trees, beech, cedar and prairie-grass have been found in the soil. Some spectacular rock-paintings discovered in the Tassili tell us more about those times. They show herds of cattle, giraffes and elephants roaming

Men swimming (Tassili rock-paintings)

the forests and prairies, beside flowing rivers and lakes.

About 4,000 years ago, the climate began to change; as it became drier, plants, animals and humans disappeared. Only the mountains, such as the Ahaggar, retained enough humidity to sustain life. But the few tribes there now lead a very different life from that of their early ancestors.

Herd of cows (Tassili rock-painting)

The Danakil Desert

Features of a salt landscape: eroded pinnacles, salt-encrusted pools of hot brine...

North of the Great Rift Valley, which divides East Africa, is a region that is not only one of the hottest, but also the most low-lying and inhospitable in the Horn of Africa: the Danakil, where the temperature is often 55°C in the shade. It is hard to believe that this desolate wasteland, between the Ethiopian plateau to the west and the Red Sea to the east, was once fertile and densely populated. Geological and climatic changes have transformed it.

The Danakil is exceptionally arid; a few sparse thorn-bushes manage to survive in those areas where the monsoon brings rain. The scenery, volcanic and unstable, consists of plateaux, faults and entrenched plains. The red, brown and green tones of molten lava, volcanic smoke-holes, and lakes of mud or warm salt water stand out against the ochre of the desert sands.

Over time, what was once a huge salt sea has evaporated to form a deep depression covered in layers of salt, which in some places are 5,000 m thick. For centuries, nomadic tribes

A vast plain of baked clay, cracked and crazed, which only experienced nomads can cross with safety.

Some 4,000 years ago these scattered outcrops of rock, which still give off sulphur fumes, lay buried beneath the waters of a vast lake. Today, Lake Abbe has almost completely dried up.

have mined and exported the salt in blocks to north-east Africa.

The Danakil is almost uninhabitable. Wildlife is scarce. Only the Afar nomads manage to survive, by pursuing what scant rainfall there is. At each stop the women put up the *toukoul*, made of woven straw mats mounted on a wooden frame.

On the left you can see an example of the *toukoul,* a type of tribal tent.

The Namib

The Cape Cross fur-seal fishes in the cold waters off the south-west coast of Africa, and along the coast of Australia.

The welwitschia, a remarkable plant found only in Namibia, can live up to 2,000 years. Every hundred years it puts out two leaves, each one 3 m long. As well as shallow lateral roots, which absorb moisture from the atmosphere, it has a tap-root which reaches down 10 m to the water-bearing bedrock below.

This desert, along the south-west coast of Africa, is one of the most ancient and most arid in the world.

Its dryness is partly due to latitude (it lies very close to the Tropic of Capricorn) and partly to the cold offshore current, the Benguela. Rainfall in the Namib is extremely rare. But each night a cold sea-breeze brings with it a

thick mist; as the sun rises the mist condenses into tiny droplets of water, which rapidly evaporate in the heat of the day. Both animals and plants have adapted to this phenomenon. The animals come out at night, in search of

any edible matter the sea-wind may have brought with it. Plants survive by storing water, and many of them are specially shaped to do this.

The scenery along this narrow coastal belt is varied. In the north, the mountains have been sculpted by the wind into weird and wonderful shapes.

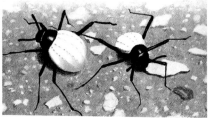

This area is well-known for the diamonds that have been found in some of the old river-beds.

Further south, the red bedrock of the Namib disappears under a sea of shifting sand-dunes, some of them more than 300 m high.

Thousands of pink flamingos flock to the Pan, a deep depression on the fringes of the desert dunes, which fills with water in the summer rains.

Darkling beetles scavenge amongst the stones for dead plant and animal material to feed on. The hard outer casing of their bodies reduces loss of water through evaporation.

Deep canyons run from the mountains to the Orange River.

The Kalahari

Colonies of meerkats, or suricates, live in underground warrens, and communicate by means of carefully regulated, high-pitched squeaks.

The Kalahari is a huge plateau some 1,000 m high, screened from rain-bearing winds by a belt of mountains. Dried-up river valleys and clay-covered basins fill briefly with water during the rains. The temperature can vary by as much as 30°C in the same

At the slightest hint of rain, brightly coloured irises pop up.

Semi-circular dwellings, made of branches loosely laced together with twigs, provide some shelter from the wind.

day. The summer rains are infrequent and leave little trace, and the rest of the year is dry.

The inhabitants of the Kalahari, the Bushmen, call themselves the *Ju Twasi*, 'people of the truth'. Descended from a very ancient race, they tend to be short, with light brown skin; they have excellent eyesight, and a keen sense of smell. Some Bushmen are still living by hunting and food-gathering. A Bushman with a poisoned arrow can bring down an antelope in full flight from a distance of 100 m. The women are the food-gatherers; they scour the desert in search of the bulbs and roots that contain water, and vegetables to cook, as well as collecting wood for fuel or to build shelters.

Apart from a few thorn-bushes and baobab trees, there is no vegetation to speak of in the Kalahari, and yet the Bushmen manage to survive in this red wilderness by hunting and gathering food.

The springbok antelope has horns in the shape of a lyre. It can travel huge distances without drinking. In the dry season, herds of springbok gather in the marshy areas on the outskirts of the desert.

At the heart of the Kalahari lies a deep red sea of rolling sand-dunes.

63

The Australian deserts

Emu

Dromedaries were introduced into Australia over a hundred years ago, to provide transport across the red sand-dunes of the Simpson Desert.

The emu is the second largest bird in the world. Emus can swim and also run very fast – up to 50 km an hour.

When threatened, the frill-necked lizard raises its ruff and lets out a loud hiss.

More than two-thirds of the Australian continent is desert. Exceptionally low rainfall is partly due to the subtropical belt of high pressure running from east to west, and partly to the coastal mountain ranges which prevent rain penetrating inland. The heart of Australia is dead: great expanses of red sand, endless beds of parched clay, shale or salt bake beneath a blazing sun. The temperature sometimes reaches 48°C in the shade. The occasional torrential downpour often does more harm than good after months of drought. The rain swiftly evaporates in the heat.

The nature of each individual desert varies according to the structure of the subsoil and the prevailing conditions.

Sturt's Stony Desert is covered in parts by a thick layer of sharp stones, or *gibber*, an Aboriginal word for stone.

The Great Sandy Desert is a huge stretch of dunes which run for miles in long parallel lines, often held fast by thorn bushes that rooted in them.

The **Victoria** and the **Gibson** are both sandy deserts, dotted with dunes. To the south is the **Nullarbor Plain**, really a limestone plateau, with cliffs dropping away steeply to the sea. The water beneath the Plain is saline.

Ayer's rock, the world's largest monolith, is the most famous landmark in Australia. It stands alone in the middle of the desert, 350 m high, with a total circumference of 9 km.

Knobs and spikes of limestone, some
no bigger than a pencil, others taller
than a house, stud the sands of the
Pinnacles National Park in
Western Australia.

The dingo, a sort of wild dog, came to Australia with the Aborigines.

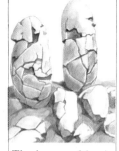

The dryness of the air and soil has preserved these dinosaur eggs for over 80 million years.

The dead-straight dunes and thorny scrub of the Simpson Desert provide shelter for a wide variety of reptiles. In other parts, clay pans attract large numbers of water-birds during the occasional wet spell, when shallow pools form.

Plants and animals have adapted to the extreme conditions. Porcupine-grass is so prickly that no animal will eat it. Many of the plants which survive in the desert are inedible.

Of the many lizards, the goanna is the largest. Some are 2 m long.

Both emus and kangaroos can live in the desert if they have access to water from time to time.

The long parallel dunes of the Simpson Desert make it difficult terrain to cross.

The Aborigines began to arrive in Australia at least 60,000 years ago. They were able to survive in the hostile conditions of the desert because of their detailed knowledge of plant and animal life, and their ability to find water. Some still know how to live like their ancestors in the wild.

In the Aborigine view of the world, Ayer's Rock (Uluru) is the dwelling place of Wanambi, the Snake Spirit, which passes judgement on all humans. In times of drought, Wanambi summons the tribes to Uluru, where they find refreshment in the pools at the foot of the Great Rock.

Wind and rain have flattened the natural contours of the landscape.

The tiny marsupial mouse feeds on insects as big as itself.

Huge flocks of budgerigars are a common sight. At dawn, thousands of these little birds fly down to drink from the pools.

The Antarctic

This grass, growing among the lichens, is able to survive the freezing cold.

Strong winds whip the snow into a blizzard, reducing visibility to less than a metre. Only specially equipped vehicles can contend with these conditions.

This massive continent, more or less centred on the South Pole, has the coldest climate in the world. The temperature never rises above 0°C, and sometimes drops to −92°C. Only the tallest mountain-peaks pierce the thick layer of ice. Very strong winds, no running water, and intense cold, make the heart of the Antarctic uninhabitable.

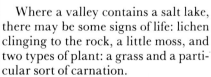

Where a valley contains a salt lake, there may be some signs of life: lichen clinging to the rock, a little moss, and two types of plant: a grass and a particular sort of carnation.

All animal life centres on the sea. None ventures far inland, where the only living organisms are minute insects such as mites and protozoans, no more than 5 mm long.

Emperor penguins seldom swim out any distance from the ice, and never venture far inland.

This scientific observation station is submerged beneath the snow, to protect it from the biting wind.

Reclaiming the desert

The desert's most treasured wealth is its oil.

These circular fields of wheat in Libya, 800 m in diameter, are watered by a long arm on rails which rotates like the hand of a watch, using water which is pumped up from 300 m underground.

In recent times, much has been done to make better use of the natural resources of the world's deserts: land, minerals, and sources of energy.

Making the desert green again

The most obvious way to make desert land fertile is to water it. But irrigation is not so simple. When the water evaporates it deposits mineral salts which often kill the crops; rivers or underground lakes of water, if tapped by too many wells and canals, may dry up altogether.

But in places the desert has bloomed. Major irrigation schemes have enabled Libya and Israel to produce and export fruit and vegetables in greater quantities than ever before.

Often the modern techniques are based on traditional methods of irrigation dating back thousands of years.

Black gold and precious minerals
Oil has been found in many desert regions: Arabia, Iraq, Texas, California...

Other deserts have yielded different treasures: silver in Mexico, copper in

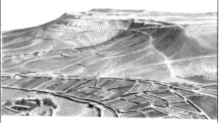

the Atacama, boron in the Mojave, diamonds in South Africa.

Even the rays of the sun, the source of all the heat, are now being used to produce electricity.

This electric power-station in the Californian Desert captures solar energy by using hundreds of individual mirrors.

In the Negev Desert, water running off the slopes is collected and directed, by a system of parapets and canals, to the cultivated land in the valley below. An area of 25 hectares will yield enough rainwater to irrigate 1 hectare of crops.

An A to Z of desert facts

Aestivation
State of semi-hibernation in which animals survive the hot, dry summer season in burrows underground.

Agave Americana
The 'century-plant', which in fact flowers every 10 years or so. Its leaves are 1.8 m long, its stalk 12 m.

Arroyos
Spanish name for deep gullies left by dried-up streams, which fill with water after rain.

Baobab tree
In the Kalahari Desert, the hard seeds of this tree can only germinate when they have been eaten by a baboon and passed out of its system in its droppings.

Barbary fig
Fleshy, edible fruit of the prickly-pear cactus.

Battuta (Ibn)
Arab geographer of the 14th century, who crossed the Sahara on his way to Timbuktu.

Bedouin
Nomadic tribesmen of the Middle East who line the floors of their spacious goatskin tents with precious carpets.

Camel
The dromedary, found from N. Africa to India, has one hump; the Bactrian, of Central Asia, has two humps, shorter legs and a thicker coat, more suited to colder conditions.

Chuckwalla
A large, harmless lizard of the American deserts. When threatened, it scuttles into a crevice in the rock and puffs itself out until so tightly wedged it cannot be pulled out.

Date
Highly nutritious fruit of the Saharan palm-tree. A Tebu proverb says that a man can live on a date for three days: the first day he eats the skin, the second day the flesh, the third day, the stone.

Desert hare
Also known as 'desert kangaroo', it can leap 5 m in one bound, and easily outdistances its pursuers.

Dune
In the silence of the night, the sand makes a strange 'singing' sound as it slips down the steep side of the dunes.

Dunhuang
A famous cave on the edge of the Gobi Desert, containing a Chinese library 1000 years old.

Empty Quarter
or Rub 'al-Khali, in southern Arabia. The largest area of continuous sand in the world, it is virtually uninhabitable.

Ephemeral
The name given to plants that only appear after rain, and otherwise remain dormant, often for several years, in the form of hardy seeds.

Erosion
What happens when top soil is washed or blown away. Sand, whipped up by the wind, acts as a powerful eroding agent in deserts.

Fech-fech
The Arabia word for the treacherous Saharan quicksands. Beneath a crisp crust, the sand is soft and powdery, so that it sinks away underfoot.

Flash floods
in the desert are caused by sudden violent rainstorms. The earth cannot absorb all the water, and soil and vegetation are often swept away.

Foggara
Arabic word for the system of tunnels used to trap underground water and channel it downhill.

Gerbils, jerboa
American gerbils and African jerboa are small rodents which are exceptionally well-adapted to desert conditions. Plants provide all the moisture they need.

Guano
A rich fertilizer made from the droppings of thousands of marine birds which congregate on barren islands off the west coast of South America. There is very little rain to wash the guano away.

Guelta
Arabic word for a water-hole which never dries up.

Halophytes
Desert plants which grow in salt soil.

Haratin
Dark-skinned inhabitants of the Saharan oases.

Harvester ants
live in nests 5 m deep in the North American deserts.

Heloderma
Gila monster, the only poisonous member of the lizard family in America;

Inselberg
From the German *Insel*, meaning island, and *Berg*, mountain. An isolated peak rising from an eroded plain.

Irrigation
Watering of desert areas by artificial means. Canals or channels are used to carry well-water to appointed sites.

Jojoba
This shrub, native to the Sonoran Desert, can survive 2 years without rain.

Joshua tree
This member of the yucca family grows 7 or 8 m tall in the Mojave Desert (USA). It can live for hundreds of years, but only under seasonal extremes of temperature.

Kum
'Sand' in Turkmen. A distinction is made between the black sands (Kara Kum), the white sands (Akkum), where nothing can survive, and the red sands (Kyzyl Kum).

Kumli
'Men of the sands' – the desert nomads of Russian Turkestan.

Lake Roger
This lake in the Mojave Desert has such a hard crust of salt that it has been used for American spacecraft landings.

Lawrence of Arabia
An English officer who lived and fought with the Arabs against the Turks. He dressed like the Arabs, in long flowing robes, and was considered a hero for his boldness and daring.

Litham
Arabic word for the veil worn by Berber nomads of the Sahara, exposing only the eyes.

Makale
Salt-market on the borders of Ethiopia, where merchants from all over northeast Africa assemble to buy salt from the nomads of the Danakil Desert.

Mesa
Mexican name for the distinctive table-top plateaux of limestone or sandstone, found in the deserts of North America.

Mirage
Optical illusion caused when rays of light bend in contact with layers of hot air.

Moors
Berber nomads living in the Sahara. Also known as 'blue men' because their skin is often stained by the dark dye in the garments they wear.

Navajos
Indians of the Arizona Desert. They

have managed to preserve their culture and traditions despite the influence of American civilization.

Niccolo Polo
Marco Polo's father, the first European to cross the deserts of Central Asia.

Oasis
A fertile area in a desert, which usually develops where there is a natural source of water.

Oxus
The old name for the Amu Darya river in Russian Turkestan. The Oxus was so wide that it took Alexander the Great's armies 5 days to cross it, using animal skins sewn together and inflated.

Pinus aristata
or the bristle-cone pine, grows in the arid White Mountains of the USA. The oldest living specimen is 4,900 years old.

Qanat
Arabic word for the underground tunnels built to channel water for irrigation. Several thousand qanats are still in use in Afghanistan and Iran.

Rul
The spirit of the sands, to be heard chuckling at travellers in distress or dying of thirst in the Sahara. Rul's 'laughter' is in fact the sound the sand makes as it shifts.

Salt
Huge areas of desert consist of salt flats, where nothing grows.

Sebkhas
Salt-encrusted depressions commonly found along the coasts of North Africa and Saudi Arabia.

Silk Road
An ancient trade route linking China with the West, travelled by caravans carrying silk and spices.

Solifugids
Long-legged desert spiders. The camel-spider has the largest jaws of any spider in the world. It is strong enough to crack and eat a darkling beetle.

Tarout
This ancient tree is a throw-back to the time when the Sahara was humid. Specimens still survive in the Tamrit (Tassili).

Tortoises
seek shelter from the heat by digging-down. They wet their heads and necks with saliva to cool themselves.

Utah
The Great Salt Lake of Utah is a remnant of a former sea, and a valuable source of potassium salts. The hard crust on the lake is used as a track for testing cars at high speed.

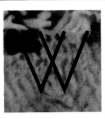

Walking Stones
These huge stones in Death Valley weigh several hundred kilos each. No one has ever seen them move, and yet they do, leaving a long trail behind them in the clay.

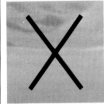

Xerophytes
Plants especially adapted to drought conditions.

Zangusk
Great exposed plain in the Kara Kum, in Russian Turkestan, constantly swept by strong winds.

Other titles in the *Discoverers* series:

Discovering Nature:
Spring
Summer
Autumn
Winter
Flowers
The Book of the Sky
The Book of Rivers

Discovering Animals:
Your Cat

Discovering History:
Clothes through the Ages
Uniforms through the Ages
Ships and Seafarers
The Book of Inventions and Discoveries
Conquerors and Invaders

Discovering transport:
The Story of Trains
Pioneers of the Air

Discovering Art:
Painting and Painters